THE
CORE
OF
FOUR

*4 Tools To Navigate Roadblocks
to Great Human Performance*

TIM PAGE-BOTTORFF, CSP, CET

outskirts
press

For Sheila.

We have faced so many challenges,

but the best part for me

is that we have faced them together.

Our challenges have become our greatest triumphs.

For this, I am grateful for my life with you.

Chapters 7-10 have no spaces after colon following #, while the rest do

Table of Contents

1) bright green, glow-in-the-dark

2) is a boom an object? if not a visible object, wouldn't be
   "amongst the streaks" or "large".
   better to switch to action-oriented statement, like
   "The sound of cannonfire boomed out from an
      artillery group stationed nearby and echoed in my
   chest. I was rattled...

3) define Scud?

4) dig deep where? hard to explain or translate.
   consider rephasing or adjusting.
      dig deep... into ourselves? lean on inner strength?
   bring out inner strength?

Foreword

At zero-three hundred hours, an alarm went off...
(recommending for ↑ action, ↓ superfluous words)

~~It was zero-three hundred hours~~ and an alarm went off in our camp outside of Khafji, Saudi Arabia. The alarm was not subtle and the duty officer for the night was screaming, "GAS GAS GAS!" I quickly put on my gas mask and full mission oriented protective posture (MOPP) gear and rushed to the underground bunker on the other side of camp. ~~I was~~ looking over the sky, ~~and~~ all I could see was an illumination of bright glow-in-the-dark green streaks across the sky. Amongst the green streaks were large pounding booms from cannon fire by the artillery group we were stationed by in the middle of the cold desert. The booms were chest rattling and could make your chest cavity echo. I was rattled and fear started to settle in at what would come next. It was an Iraqi SCUD missile attack that sounded the alarm and it was uncertain if there were any Army Patriot missile pods in the area. The Army Patriots were the short-range missiles that were solely responsible for taking down a majority of the SCUD missiles that Iraq ~~would send~~ sent over to Saudi Arabia or Israel during the 1990 Persian Gulf War. The green streaks in the sky were tracer rounds from ~~ground to air~~ space machine gun nests from our camp perimeter. We were on high alert and ~~have~~ had been for over three days when the attack occurred. I ~~ended up getting~~ was drawn for ~~berm~~ security duty and had to stand watch on the berm facing Kuwait at the border. My Platoon Leader ~~at the time~~ reminded ~~me and~~ my berm mate that ~~we were all~~ everyone was exhausted, ~~and were~~ but the camp was on high alert and that we and I needed to dig deep to ensure that we would not fall asleep. Roughly around zero-four hundred hours, my berm mate and I decided to stay awake together and we would build a quasi-fox hole to help keep our body profile below the berm apex, not to mention, keeping busy to stay awake. The fox-hole was finished within an hour and I decided that I would take first watch and my berm mate would take first rest. It was really comfortable.

Sergeant Cole counted 25 seconds while he stood there watching two marines sleeping in a fox hole on top of a berm. He was pissed. He took both of the Marine's weapons with bayonets fixed and threw them, muzzle first, into the soft desert sand until they sunk in. After the weapons sunk in he kicked them further into the sand until the weapon's butt stocks barely showed. He pulled both of the Marines down from the top of the berm and made them both dig a six-foot trench respectively. The six-foot trench they dug symbolized a grave if they fell asleep and were attacked. The two Marines would be the first to hypothetically die and would have never had a chance to challenge the infiltrators or sound an alarm.

To this day I am still angry at myself for falling asleep at my post. I cannot believe that I put my entire camp at risk for what I did. I swear I wasn't going to fall asleep and that I would do everything in my power to make sure my berm mate would be safe. Falling asleep at your post was punishable by court marshal. "Quit My Post Only When Properly Relieved." It was one of our Marine Corps General Orders or covenants if you will, albeit 25 seconds and however much time it took Sgt. Cole to ascend to our position, which could have been more than a minute. It was a supreme lack of discipline and terrible Marine Corps human performance. Even after all the discipline training I received before arriving in the Persian Gulf I still had a serious problem.

Looking back, it is clear, now more than ever. I needed the motivation to swing me in the right direction. Discipline is great, but you could be the most disciplined person in the world and make a major performance mistake. I needed more. I was lucky. My berm-mate was lucky. My camp was lucky. I relied on my adrenaline to keep me awake that night. That night, January 18, 1991, in Operation Desert Storm there were no enemies near our camp and they were at least a couple of hundred kilometers away. Still, with my absent mindedness, had the situation been different or in a jungle, or dug in a fox hole in Vietnam, my entire platoon and attachment could have been casualties, or even worse dead. Until now I have never shared that story with anyone except for Sgt. Cole (who witnessed it) and of course, now you.

Safety and health is not a profession I jumped out of my mother's womb with excitement for. I mean, when I was born the safety profession never crossed my mind. As a matter of fact, when most 7 year-olds dream of what they want to be when they get older they probably don't have safety identified as one of those awesome, dream jobs. I wasn't any different. I was what I considered to be normal (I didn't know what normal was). I wanted to be a firefighter and a baseball player. I got to live these dreams growing up because I got temporary orders in the Marine Corps to be a firefighter and I also played baseball for the Marine Corps for a whole year. Getting paid to play baseball was a no-brainer. I couldn't turn it down. Later-on in my career I ended up being a Captain on an industrial fire brigade and it fulfilled many of my childhood aspirations. Eventually, I started training OSHA compliance classes and voila! With no pun intended, I fell into Safety. I became a safety professional. I was pretty damn excited about it too.

This book is somewhat a download of multiple experiences throughout my many years in the safety and health universe. The best part about this book is that with great safety performance you get even better quality, productivity and eventually profit. Improve one, and you can ultimately improve them all. If you don't have any, you will have what I call high potential to become a culture creator or a company failure. The Core of Four can get you to where you need to be, a culture creator. This book will define the "getting there." Increasing performance is the key but understanding that there is no magical performance pill to increase your performance is more important. Perhaps, the magical pill is you.

I have found that over the years, if I wanted to get something accomplished, I have to be the one to motivate myself and eventually perform all the follow up to ensure, well, frankly; *it gets done!* I bring this up because to me it was a sudden reality, but it wasn't nothing new. In other words, I didn't invent how to get things done. I was motivated by a great many things, but ultimately, I wanted to take care of one thing. Sheila. I mean, how dependent was I on Sheila, my wife, to connect the mundane dots between decision-making? I see global thoughts and most of the time have difficulty in reaching milestones (the dots in a connect-a-dot image). Sheila is fantastic at perceiving the details and reaching milestones. Some of the comparisons in this book will be her view against mine. I will refer to this wisdom as what would Sheila do (WWSD?) By having the WWSD conversation we will begin to understand how she achieves such success in her detail-oriented mind and in my mind-minutia. What I might consider to be minutia might be very important and in the past I have let my ego rule them out. In other words, the minutia wasn't important. Now, over time, I have learned to listen to the minutia but it *was* a lesson and I thought, *this should be for everyone.* Minutia is now considered gold in my mind and I thank Sheila for being consistent and constantly motivating me to see it. The Core of Four was developed with my intense passion to help other people. I know I needed help and Sheila is always helping me and now I want to help others get better too. Sheila convinced me to do better. She was an upgrade to my life. I am in debt to her, I owe her my life.

Acknowledgments

I began my career with Sheila at my side and she is the first person I would like to thank. Sheila, without you, there would be no success nor would there be love and caring without your intuitive guidance. You are the straightest arrow I know, and I owe you my life. I want to also thank my children, Eli, Courtney and Camryn. These three are the foundation of my will to achieve success. I can only succeed when I know they are succeeding. In my early twenties, coming home and sitting down to watch Disney movies after a late third shift with Courtney was incredible bonding time. Camryn, my youngest, developed the original image of coming down to earth for the cover of this book. Even though there were several iterations of the design for the cover, it was her amazing imagination that was responsible for me to come down to earth and understand that my perception isn't everyone's reality. Eli for bringing great joy to this family. My Dad, Curt, who has been a pillar strong and true never wavering. Kathi for providing grounded love and a humble respect for family. I also want to thank my brothers, Jason and Ryan for always giving and being real cool people. Mom and Steve for helping in times of need. Ashlee, one of the "coolest" people I know

I have many others to thank, but that would take the rest of this book, so I narrowed a few down to those that have made the greatest impact on my life, career and future. First, I must thank Jeff Buntrock, Tom Steeves, and Ellie Vargas for giving me a chance at a job all those years ago at Motorola and having confidence in me, Chris Hansen and Jeff Heaps you know why. Two great United States Marines, Gunnery Sergeant John Pythian and Staff Sergeant Ryan Stiles for pushing me over the hump during those dreaded few Marine Corps months. Senior Drill Instructor Sergeant Jackson who knew I could do 20 pull ups- I surely didn't think I could. Perry Morris for getting me to jump ship. Brian Weatherly and Cara Garry for all the intense valuable discussions. Milissa, Melissa, Tony M, John B, and any other former employee who advanced their careers after being under my management. Cari Elofson for equality mentorship and guidance in a hostile environment. Eric Garcia for being a really good friend and sounding board. Ray Prest for reviewing the manuscript. Jack Jackson for being a great friend and life coach. Kevin Cobb for always being the antithesis in a good way and our long conversations into the wee hours of the night with smoke and fire. Gary, Danny, and Ruth for being true professionals, mentoring and guiding me to always do better; you are my best friends and my favorite team ever! David Threlfall for providing serious, stark, difficult feedback that was sincerely needed. Barb Tait for your strong leadership, incredible-contagious- energy, stability and belief in family, Don Wilson for showing me slower is the new fast, Kelley Norris for holding the lamp-always seemingly in the darkest corridors, and Larry Wilson for being a genius and helping me through this book writing process. Lastly, I wish to thank the many friends on social media for your votes on the book cover. Through this process, I learned a lot about design and marketability. I wish I could thank more and most of you know who you are, so this goes out to everyone that I have ever worked with, talked to, mentored, or listened to; I say thank you very much! You have made a great impact on me and the development of this book.

CHAPTER 1

Meeting Larry Wilson

I met Larry Wilson at the 2002 Southwest Safety Congress in Mesa, Arizona. Larry was the keynote speaker and things were rather crazy that week because I was on the Advisory Council for the Arizona Chapter of the National Safety Council. I told Perry Morris, a former employee and super great friend, that I want to be like him (Larry) when I get older. His charisma and charm while on stage was amazing and he was a decent speaker on top of being a great entertainer. During Larry's presentation, still on printed transparency sheets, he showed us things that I already knew but didn't quite see it like Larry had organized it. During the week of the conference I found myself rushed and super frustrated and Larry comes in and delivers this fantastic presentation about how rushing and frustration causes Critical Errors™. I was immediately reflecting on the week and the "Critical Errors™" I made. I turned without looking first, I bumped my shin on a table at the convention center, and

I stubbed my toe on my household coffee table. I am sure there were many others, but these were the critical errors I could remember. Larry is the author of SafeStart the most successful, global, safety consultative process ever. Let me say it again, *ever*. After I met Larry, I thought there is no way that SafeStart could be that easy. I told Larry, "This has to be just common sense." Little did I know, I was the "skeptical safety engineer." Larry replied, "Do people make common sense common practice?" That's when I was hooked. I started using SafeStart almost immediately. The *Four* States, The *Four* Critical Errors, The *Four* Critical Error Reduction Techniques™. These elements of four kept popping up as prime motivators to get better with injury reduction, and improving my workplace performance. Naturally, SafeStart helped with the workplace performance, but ultimately it helped me out everywhere I went. On the road, at home *and* at work.

Larry eventually started to write a book discussing the decision- making process from the inside out. This was pretty cool to me seeing the process of book writing. No, I was not motivated to write a book, but I was intrigued by the idea of four. I kept seeing the number everywhere. I would have a hard time convincing Las Vegas that the number four is the new number seven, but people gamble every day of their life. They take risk, negotiate risk, mitigate risk and even laugh at risk. Some do better than others, but I succeed more so when I ask myself a simple question each day before the day begins, "Have I MAPPED out my day?" What **M**otivates me?

Who am I *Accountable* to? Am I *Practicing Perfectly?* Do I *Exercise Discipline?* M.A.P.P.ED.

Four ideas that people wrestle with every day. 4 steps to navigate roadblocks to great human performance, *The Core of Four.*

CHAPTER 2

Pain Does Not Discriminate.

*"Life is pain, anyone who says different
is selling something."*

William Goodwin

When I first thought about pain and its inherent lack of discrimination I was at a conference in Anaheim, California and I was having a discussion with a good friend of mine, Eric Garcia, about the difference between Kobe Bryant and Michael Jordan and who was the "best." In the beginning the conversation was really subdued but eventually turned into a heated debate. This conversation was so out of bounds, that we started discussing the difference between black and white, Filipino and Hispanic, the Phoenix Suns vs. The L.A. Lakers and all of the sudden it hit me in the face. Even though we were joking, we were discriminating against people that weren't there to defend themselves. So, naturally, questions started popping up in my mind that night. Does everyone discriminate? Does Michael or Kobe discriminate? Does Steve Nash Discriminate?

At the time, these questions kept popping up in my mind, Steve Nash played for the Phoenix Suns and was injured by Tim Duncan in the NBA Western Conference Semifinals with a gash on the bridge of his nose. That game changed the course of the entire playoffs for the Suns and they ended up losing that series with the Spurs. It dawned on me, does pain discriminate? The answer is no. Pain does not care who you are, where you are, what you do, what you do for a living, what you do for a hobby, or who you decide to marry. See a trend? Pain does not discriminate. Ultimately, pain might force you to change who you are or what you do (habits), change where you live (moving from the Middle East to Lincoln, Nebraska), or change your hobbies (downhill skiing to knitting). Pain does not care who you are, what you do or where you live. Severe pain will remind you of the past because we often never forget it. The Occupational Safety and Health Administration (OSHA) has many federal regulations that are required to be imposed, enforced and followed. Usually, when I have discussions about the OSHA regulations it typically results in statements like, "the regulations should be printed in red ink." Red ink would signify that all the regulations were written simply because there were fatalities or serious injuries which required some form of a regulation to mitigate it." "Red ink equals blood." "The regulations are written in blood."

In the example with OSHA, pain had a lot to do with the generation of many different regulations. Obviously, pain didn't care who died or where it happened. Pain is an incredible motivator when it comes to change. I have known Larry to ask questions like, "Have you ever slammed your finger in a car door?" Everyone he asks would always raise their hands. Some would raise both hands immediately to signify that they emphatically have had too many finger pains. The irony is when Larry asks, "so, of those that have slammed a finger in a car door, who has slammed a finger in a car door twice, three times?" There are hardly any hands that go up. Pain does a great job of keeping our hands/fingers out of the line of fire. Pain motivates and does not discriminate.

In the safety world there are many different forms of pain. There could be physical pain, mental pain or pain in a business. Pain in business is usually akin to upset conditions. A machine goes down, overtime compensation, etc. These are usually similar to indirect costs for business. I was teaching a class for a major automotive customer in Anna, Ohio and the Business Unit Leader made sure that I let the students out on time, not early, not late, but on time. He also reminded me that if I let the associates out late, that it would cost me more than they paid for my services. I was motivated to let the associates out on time and more importantly, it was the customers experience with lost time (business pain) that really screamed out at me. How much are you willing to bet that they had a past class that let out late and caused some production headaches? Pain motivates and does not discriminate.

Most of us have experienced mental pain, and for some, way too much. I can create a massively long list here, but to narrow it down to the most common: high school breakups, cut from an athletic team, disappointed parents, a parental divorce, moving to a different school, not making the grade, missed auditions, etc…

Just like soft tissue injuries that leave permanent scars or wounds, mental pain can leave their permanent scars or wounds too. The experience of a divorce could be traumatic and leave a permanent scar. My parents are divorced and at the time of the divorce I was a wreck. My father was the only thing stable to me and for him to vacate the family was really painful. The pain endured for a year until he returned to town and then the scar remained but the pain subsided. I was able to move away from the pain because my mind was on other things. Music, friends and my brother Jason were the reasons why I was able to move away from pain. Jason helped me because I was responsible for watching Jason and it forced me to grow up and pay better attention to the things that were really important. At the time of the divorce Jason was 6 years old and with my mom trying to support us, it was my responsibility to feed, watch and make sure Jason did his homework, amongst many other things.

My parent's divorce was painful, but it sure did provide clarity on the most important things in life. The most important thing to me is family. This motivation is superior to anything else in my life. Unfortunately, it was pain that provided clarity. I must also add an additional motivator and some information about my Grandpa Bob. Grandpa Bob was always the center of attention, but he was a big believer in family. I got to see Grandpa Bob once or twice a year when I was grow-ing up. It was one of those things knowing that we would be going to Grandpa Bob's where I would get ready to go 4-5 hours before we were actually going to leave. Before the divorce, all my dad had to say was, "we are going to Grandpa Bob's tomorrow." You want to see someone get ready in a flash? Well, that was me. I loved my Grandpa Bob. He always wanted all the family members together during all the holidays and everything else that would usually bring families together. Grandpa Bob lost his wife way too early in life to complications from a previous surgery. I never met Grandma Amy. This pain could cause someone to grasp on to things that are still around like children and other family members. I learned from Grandpa Bob that love and life are so important that once they leave you, only then can you recognize the pain. Pain motivates and does not discriminate.

Here is one final motivator from pain and an experience that has happened in my family more than once. I have a biological father who according to my mother left us when I was born. The father that I refer to in my life and in this book is the one who raised me (Curt). He will never be anything less than my father, a great father at that. Part of the reason I have a hyphenated last name is because of this man. My mom and dad married when I was 4 years old and they were together for over a year before they were married, so as far as memories go, he was and will always be my father. A feeling of abandonment was a nerve never touched. I never fully had this feeling but it surfaced when my "man I call dad" and mom got divorced. It was almost uncontrollable, these feelings of abandonment. In other words, a lot of pain surfaced and I had to manage it all at age 13. I would almost suggest that it was too young of an age for anyone to endure. I mentioned that this has happened too often, and it has. I too had a son when I was young and for many different circumstances, I was asked to sign over parental rights. And so I did. I strugled with it. But now I was no better than my bio-dad. I, too, did the same thing he did to me. I abandoned my son Eli. At the time, I was only interested in what was best for Eli. I never realized that these actions would harm anyone until I went through them for myself. There is no other way to put it in the eyes of a child. I know, because it happened to me. Of course, when I signed over the rights, I was only thinking about what was best for him. There was so much pain and I wanted the vicious cycle to stop now. I owe Eli the world and no words can explain my decision from his point of view. Ironic, because no words could explain what my bio-dad did to me. Here is the kicker, when he turned 18, Eli searched for me and is now a huge part of this family. I could not have wished for anything better than to have Eli a part of this family.

Ironically, I have not had any motivation to look for my bio-dad, there is too much pain for me. But I have learned a lesson from Eli. Regardless the amount of pain associated with abandonment, he sought me out. Incidentally, my bio-dad has already reached out to me to extend a hand of sorrow and remorse, to a pain he knows he contributed to. Pain motivates but does not discriminate.

The body wants to repair wounds, so does the mind. Pain can be used as a positive motivator to help us get beyond the scars and deep wounds. As Larry said, hardly anyone has closed a car door on a finger a second or third time. We have learned because pain is a huge motivator, more importantly, pain hurts too much to have to relive over and over again. We can all do a better job by just letting go of so much pain. Most of the pain is a derivative of the past. The pain of our past can shape us, change us or destroy us, but in the infinite words of Walt Disney, "we must keep moving forward."

CHAPTER 3

Roadblock Number 1 And The Doors of Opportunity-Pride and Ego

"Your ego can become an obstacle of your own work,
but only if you start believing in your greatness."

-Spock

Before I can effectively explain the Core of Four, I think it prudent to explain what makes the Core of Four malfunction in the first place. Consider the following road blocks: Ego/ pride, convenience (short cuts), temptation, mal-perception (low self- esteem). The title of this chapter might be a bit misleading, however these roadblocks could be considered doors of opportunity if treated correctly. For example, traveling consultants that get easy, repeat business usually know that their services are top notch. Loosely translated, these consultants know they are good and their pay is directly proportionate to their services. This is a marketing door of opportunity and not a roadblock. Word of mouth marketing will work for you when you deliver what you say you will deliver. When the customer is happy with your services, they usually tell you great job, but the hidden agenda is they tell their friends and other potential customers that you were amazing. If the consultant internalizes the comments and absorbs the "at-a-boys/girls" the ego could take over and the doors of opportunities close immediately. Now we are staring at a roadblock. This is not to be confused with Freud's Ego.

In my research to better understand the ego, I had to realize first that I had some problems with ego and pride early on in my career. I used to think that I was this prodigious consultant that no one could touch. I was on the other end of the spectrum when it came to being humble. My ego was fueled by customers always asking (requesting my services by name) for me, and I was not building my employees to be better at what they do. Yes, I had 8 consultants report to me and I was more concerned about wanting to be in front of clients and hearing the customer tell me that I was the best and I was the one they wanted. One of the biggest roadblocks I ever had was my own personal ego.

I started doing this presentation called "The Humor in Safety" several years ago. The presentation was not about comedy but how to spruce up your presentations to better fulfill what the students wanted as opposed to what the speaker/instructor wanted. I would always get to this point in the presentation where I would tell the attendees, "the minute you feel like you've practiced enough, it is time to do more work and practice even more." This was a huge slap in the face. Ultimately, I would finish the presentation with these words, "once you realize you are there for the students and not yourself, that is when you will truly find your calling!" I finally realized that I was not in front of my clients to fulfill my own ego needs, I was there to fulfill the needs of the students or customers who needed my services. As soon as I realized this, my quality of training and services changed and more importantly, I changed. I am not there for me, I am there for them. What a concept.

In 2000-2005 while I was working for a local Arizona consulting company, I would always complain to Sheila about the owners and all of their empty promises to me for partial ownership. She knew that I was unhappy and the workload was changing along with me. After hearing me complain night after night, Sheila finally blurted out, "why don't you just quit?" I started to think was this a statement to get me to shut up or to actually get me to quit? My reply was a moment of growth for me. I replied, "but the consultants need me there to be a buffer, they need me." Being a buffer was a reference I used in regards to protecting the employees from the owner and his fly-by-the-seat-of his pants ownership decisions. I was lying to myself and Sheila was right. I needed to go. Perry Morris, who at the time, was one of my consultants, told me to go to work for Larry and Safestart and I struggled with making that decision. My biggest roadblock was my clients, my consultants, my ego...who would feed my ego? I was compromising my sanity by working at a job that just didn't give me what I needed. Now, trust me, the job was giving me what I wanted, but not what I needed. As my ego quickly turned into pride, I felt that I would be really good on my own. The door of opportunity opened for me to start my own business and to start working for SafeStart. This door was opened because of an error (roadblock) that was solely contributed to my ego. Among other mistakes I made prior to my departure from the Arizona consulting company I was working for, I was finally humbled to realize the safety business is about saving lives *and* not filling in the gaps my ego always created. Interesting concept, to change the way you think. In an intense conversation, I was once told by my oldest daughter Courtney that if you want to see change, you must first look in the mirror for the change. And so I did. I opened a door and removed the roadblocks. Working as a selfless consultant was now more important to me to see people being mentored and coached by what you had to provide as opposed to striving for more and more attention. I did it!

Barb Tait has an incredible vision as is recognized by me and everyone else at SafeStart to be one of the most selfless persons I have ever met. When I first met Barb, I was just set aside to see someone care so much for people. I didn't know that existed. My military background influenced me to care about the "Corps" before all else. This was a tough concept to depart from. The mentality Barb displays towards her company and her employees was equally a sharp departure from what I was used to. But to sentiment or echo what my Grandpa Bob used to say, family is more important than anything. Well, so is the family away from home. Immediately Barb made me feel like I was part of the family-the Electrolab[1] Family. I never had that feeling at a job before, and now I knew it was possible. It was a feeling of Pride.

Here is a better explanation, it meant so much to me to be able to work for a place that is much larger than life and to take part of a vision that was congruent with my own, delivered a huge amount of pride. Proud to belong, proud to deliver a message of saving lives, these were just a couple of examples of "good" pride. I experienced similar feelings before when I started volunteering for my local chapter (The Arizona Chapter) of the American Society of Safety Engineers (Now Professionals). I knew it was volunteer work and I didn't see the instant return on investment to my time commitment. However, I felt a sense of belonging and other chapter members encouraging me to do more and more. I joke about it now, but when I first started volunteering, my mentor Mike Cook told me volunteering for the ASSE is like a caveman dragging his wife or child with their ponytails. Although, I admit that I never felt like I was dragged into the world of volunteerism, it is funny to look back at Mike's analogy. I mean, Mike kind of volun-told me to be a committee chair without me even thinking about it, I said yes.

---

[1] Electrolab is the parent company that owns the SafeStart Product and provides many other services. Electrolab resides in Belleville, Ontario, Canada and has been in business for nearly 40 years. Each employee has a sense of belonging to a family away from home.

It is important that you get a sense of pride which, comes mostly in positive forms. It could also cause some road-blocks and the doors of opportunity will close on you so fast, you won't know how to react.

The best example I can give you is a personal experience I witnessed with regard to growth at the same Arizona consulting firm I was a Director for. I was responsible for oversight of 8 consultants, business development, and being personally billable 85% of my total work time. It was one too many balls to juggle. I think you can get the picture. I wanted to be so involved in everything from making decisions to getting right in front of the customer. What I didn't realize was all of these responsibilities were self-inflicted. The company really only wanted what was best for me and, simultaneously, the future of the company. What was best for me (at least what I thought was best) was a conflict because I was too proud to admit it. I had a problem with focusing on one thing and do-ing that one thing really good, as opposed to three or four things simultaneously, barely mediocre. What I have learned from this experience and why I must share it with you is for a couple of reasons. First, what I thought was the company trying to take responsibilities away from me was really them saying we want what is best for you and the company. What I heard (my translation with too much pride) was you are terrible at these things and we are going to take them away from you. I was blinded by pride, and my ego was crushed to boot. Finally, since moving away from the consulting firm I have taken advantage of previous experiences and owning my own consulting firm has made me see the errors I made due to pride and ego. I would be lying to you if I said that I am completely pride and ego free in regards to road-blocks. I would admit though, I am working on it on a daily basis and it is tough, but I really believe that making headway can only begin by admitting to it first. Psychologists everywhere suggest, if you want to change, identifying the roadblock is important. What is more imporant is to cut yourself some slack.[2] A huge advantage in performance is to recognize this as a potential problem. Making pride and ego doors of opportunities open up for you is a much better way to go than to have them turn into roadblocks. The Core of Four is a great tool to help open those doors of opportunity.

2   Psychologists everywhere would include many sources. Here is one for you to review: Mary Hartwell-Walker Ed.D 7 Steps to Changing a Bad Habit

CHAPTER 4

Roadblock Number 2
The Doors of Opportunity-
Convenience

The man on the TV says, "it's the fourth quarter and there are 2 minutes left." Your favorite team has the ball and they are about to score to win the game. Faintly, you hear your young child screaming and your wife/husband says that you need to go get some milk right now! I think you are very familiar with the tone in which they deliver this message. Decision time it is! Do you say I will wait, go to the local convenience store, or take your time and go the grocery store?

It most certainly is a struggle, but after polling over 500 attendees at my training sessions over 75% admit they would go to the convenience store. They would prefer to pay more money by going to the local convenience store, which would get them home perhaps before the end of the game. They know if they go to the grocery store it would take longer to get back and they certainly want to get away from the screaming.

I know making the decision to go to the local convenience store is not a difficult one, but we don't normally see the long-term impact immediately. Long-term ramifications suggest that you would ultimately save money going to the grocery store, but money at the moment of truth (screaming child, wife/husband in need) is never a concern or even a forethought. As a matter of fact, the frustration with having to leave from your important game and hearing the screaming child, most certainly *made* you go to the convenience store instead of the grocery store. Why do you suppose 7-11 and Circle K are successful? They attract those who need convenience versus the long-term benefits of saving money at the grocery store.

You might be wondering why I bring up convenience as a door of opportunity. Really, the decision-making process in its traditional sense does not discuss ease or convenience. It does discuss people decide things based on ease, though. I get it, whatever is easiest is best. No! Decisions of convenience are usually made out of haste or impatience. Yes, there is a difference between haste and impatience. I have both. Haste is just simply being in a hurry and impatience is a combination of haste (rushing) and frustration. I am mostly impatient while driving and I have made some mistakes when I was impatient with other drivers. Let me give you the perfect example. During the winter months, while living in Phoenix, it brings in all different kinds of retired snowbirds from out of the state. I do not judge them, but they do have a tendency to drive under the speed limit. I mean, way under the speed limit. In my observation they always appear to be lost. My roadway observations always include my opinion of other drivers, and my destination is obviously more important than theirs. So now, impatience settles in and I am now going to increase my risk so I can accomplish fulfilling my need in getting to my more important destination. Out of convenience, I made a decision instantly and yes, I used to do this all the time. This example is a closed door of opportunity, and it was out of convenience to me. I could certainly make a decision thinking more about the long-term impact instead of the impulse of impatience.

I know the tone of the previous example was full of sarcasm but let me give you a real-life example that could of had long term implications not just to me but to my family too.

My younger daughter Camryn needed a ride to a rehearsal for a musical she was performing in. So, my wife and I were going to make a day of it. Once we dropped her off, we were going to have lunch and hang out together. My time with her was valuable because I travel and when I am home, I hoard the time I can spend with my family. Traffic going to the rehearsal space was very slow and I was worried Camryn would be late to rehearsal. Impatience settled in quickly. When we pulled into the drive way of the rehearsal building there was a car zooming perpendicular in front of us and if I hadn't slammed on my brakes, we would have had a collision in a private parking lot. After I stopped, the other driver was so startled to see my bumper he also stopped. Our eyes connected and I immediately let him know how I felt. I threw up some gestures that would end up not making my wife very happy. He threw his hands in the air as if to say he was sorry. I wasn't having it! So upset and still in a hurry, I wanted to get in front of the startled driver. He had already parked and I just realized that we were in front of Camryn's rehearsal space. It just so happened that he, too was dropping off his son who was a co-actor with Camryn in the same musical. Ok, now I felt like a total heal.

The incident went away and I haven't seen the guy a second or a third time. I would have been too embarrassed to talk to him. The long-term ramifications could have been horrific for Camryn and it wasn't a thought that crossed my mind at the time. My wife volunteered as the President of the Board too, and I would have put her in an akward position, mostly due to embarrassment, but who wants that? I know I don't. A short-term decision to get angry at a driver out of my impatience of being late and almost getting into an accident. It was easy to blame him for the near collision, but that is too convenient. The reality of it all is I need to work harder at my impatience and stop looking for the easy blame for a potential error I made, mostly in judgment, but an error with more long-term ramifications than short term benefits.

CHAPTER 5

Roadblock Number 3, The Doors of Opportunity- Temptation

Oh the joys of sugar, dairy and gluten. I enjoy all of them, too much. My life is full of temptation and controlling it is not easy. Recently Sheila has asked me to work on my eating behavior and for the better part of our marriage I have mostly refused. I know I am getting older and I used to be in super shape. Most of my "in-shape" moments were when I was in the Marine Corps, but as soon as I got out I weighed 230 pounds within the first year. Compare that to 196 pounds when I was in. 34 additional pounds can wreak havoc on a body that is not prepared to handle it.

Losing weight has been a long battle for so many people. Even when most people lose weight they almost always put it back on. Those who keep it off are always committed to keep it off. *They do whatever it takes to keep it off.* They work. They work really hard. It takes work to do it and it isn't easy. With convenience and temptation together, it is a double whammy and you would most certainly fail at losing weight if you succumbed to both. With the Core of Four and while writing the book, I have found that I could take a dent out of each one slowly if I start to work at it. I mean, I *really* love chocolate and I *really* want to lose weight.

My temptation with chocolate and sugar started at an early age. We never had it around the house, but when we were able to get it, I would devour it and impatiently wait for the next holiday. Because, that was when we would always get sweets. I was hooked after my first peanut butter cup. My Grandpa Bob used to spoil me too. He would always give me some kind of chocolate. My mom always wondered why I always wanted go to Grandpa Bob's house.

Because a doctor told you, might be too late. During a routine visit to the V.A. for my annual physical I had a high level of ferritin in my liver. Ferritin is blood cell protein that contains iron. Too high or too little iron can cause your liver to function improperly. Normal levels of ferritin in males is 12-300 ng/mL and 12-150 ng/mL for females. My ferritin level was 469 ng/mL. There are a couple of ways to remove ferritin from the body but one of the ways was an absolute no vote for me. That way was bloodletting. I didn't want to do that and the other way was something I was willing to do. I was forced to change my diet. I met with a nutritionist and viola! I changed my eating habits. I had to remove sugar, dairy and gluten from my diet. No more, chocolate, candy or bread. No more cereal and milk in the morning. You get the picture. I had to make a change to my temptation because a doctor told me. I know it motivated me to change, but it should have never come to this point. Use temptation as a trigger to change, not as a crutch to continue the undesirable behavior. I eventually dropped my level of ferritin in the body and lost 28 pounds in the process.

Temptation became a roadblock and I started to see it, especially when I wanted to start losing weight. Eating chocolate doesn't help in losing weight, but in moderation maybe, and understanding the benefits of certain types of chocolate. Sheila explained that different percentages of dark chocolate are a healthier option. Identifying the ability to take baby steps was the first step. I had to identify personal milestones and I was motivated to lose weight. So my second step was to ask Sheila for help and she stepped up huge! Sheila told me getting into shape started in the kitchen. In reference to the kitchen, you really had to be cognizant of what you eat. This was a huge undertaking for me. I am so used to traveling and eating whatever was down the street. Chopping vegetables was out of line. I mean, I used to tell people I was allergic to vegetables and at times, I would tell people that I don't eat things that grow out of the ground. I didn't realize what I was keeping from my body, who was screaming for all of that veggie goodness.

Step two, eat more vegetables, or at least attempt it. Step three less sugar. Whoa! Wait! What? You can't be serious. I certainly didn't have a temptation for vegies. But I needed them to prepare my body to lose weight. Whatever am I going to do? Sheila said, don't worry I got you covered. For a while she made different things to see if they were palatable to make my taste buds accept them. Some things worked and some things *didn't* work. She worked hard to help me. I mean she would shred cauliflower to make a mashed potato mixture that was all cauliflower and no potato. It was good. I started to eat more salads and she incorporated a vegatble pill that I took twice a day. These pills had 5-7 servings of veggies in them.

I remember many discussions with Sheila and I would complain sometimes about the food. I mean I am eating pizza now with cauliflower crust and I have tried quinoa as a rice replacement. I used to spend more time complaining and refusing than just trying and eating. The roadblock of temptation really caused me to make poor decisions. Theodore Roosevelt said, "I dream of men taking the next step and not of men who think of the next 1000 steps." We all want to lose the 10-20 pounds now and not two months from now. Take the steps required to get there not the giant leap. If there were a giant leap to lose weight instantly, wouldn't we all have tried it already? If it weren't for the V.A. hospital and the Nutritionist, perhaps I would have never changed. Remove the temptation to bring you down before your goals, or you will lose an open door of opportunity. Don't wait for the Doctor to tell you, it may be too late.

CHAPTER 6

Roadblock Number 4
The Doors of Opportunity
– Perception and Self Esteem
(Blame and Judgment)

"Why should we worry about what others think of us?
Do we have more confidence in their opinions than
we do our own?"

– Brigham Young

In my experience, this roadblock starts at an early age. I will base this chapter solely on my personal experiences with close friends, family and myself. I cannot speak for all the folks that I have met that were having perception or low self-esteem challenges. However, I can speak to my own. I have had severe lessons in humility and triumphs in overcoming usually unattainable challenges. Early on in childhood development, I attended a new school every summer. From Kindergarten to my senior year in high school, there was new friends, new locations, new everything. The longest I ever stayed anywhere is the town I call my hometown. The town is south of Champaign, Illinois and is 10 miles from Eastern Illinois University. The landmarks mentioned are important because the University of Illinois is in Champaign and most people can relate to its location and the other is Eastern Illinois University (EIU), which is located in Charleston, Illinois and is the University that a quarterback from my favorite football team attended. The team is the Cowboys and the quarterback is Tony Romo. This is significant to this chapter later on.

The town I call my hometown is Mattoon, Illinois. I learned a majority of my young life lessons in Mattoon, a town of 20,000 people. I also learned most of my poor self-esteem lessons in this town and a majority of it was due to my own perception of the people, community, and more importantly the perception of myself. Previous to moving to Mattoon, Illinois I lived in 2 St Louis suburbs and 5 different towns throughout Indiana and was too young to develop any poor perceptions or potential bad behavior. I went to Kindergarten in East St. Louis, Illinois. 1st grade was a little further east in a town called Mascoutah, Illinois and in second grade we moved to Indiana to start the 5-town tour. My dad was a manager for a local discounted department store based in Columbus, Indiana called Danner's Discount Department Store (3-D as it was known in the region). We went from Seymour, Indiana to Greenfield, Portland,

Rushville and Warsaw before we landed in Mattoon, Illinois. From Kindergarten to 6th grade I attended 7 different elementary schools. I just thought moving was a way of life and that each child I met must have moved as much or more than my family and I did. I was dead wrong. When I moved to Mattoon, I learned that we were the "weird ones." Although my perception at ages 9 and 10 were that everyone moved around as much as I did. I was closed minded about the truth. Most people don't move around as much as we did. I believed that this was the gospel and there was no other way. Eventually I realized that this was not always good, and finally, I started to believe that I was weird for moving all the time. When we moved around in Indiana, we moved from one trailer park to another. There was a time we lived in an apartment, but for the most part it was a trailer. We would pull off the skirting, pressure fill the tires and hire someone to pull the trailer to the next location. I have never lived in a house per se during my grade school years. All the folks I became perennial friends with always had houses, nice things, and you guessed it, made me envious. I could never learn to be content. We finally ended up in Mattoon with the trailer. What a life I led, I mean who gets to travel each summer to a new city, roll glasses in newspaper and tape up the drawers? We taped drawers when we moved instead of packing boxes. The drawers held our private effects like clothes and it was easier to tape the drawers shut instead of packing. I vaguely remember packing glass and things that could shatter, but for the most part we taped everything and off we went.

I perceived quite a few "different" things before ever moving to Mattoon, but I was in for a rude awakening. It came like a massive storm too. When we left Warsaw to head to Mattoon, I was playing in the city championships for the Leesburg Orioles baseball team. We ended up winning that championship and were elevated to state championships but our move to Mattoon took precedence and that state championship series never took place for me. I was resentful for having to leave but I knew I had to get back to tape the dressers because it was that time of year. 6 hours later after following the "wide-load" signs we arrived at the trailer park our trailer would see as its final resting place. A couple of weeks later I was enrolled into the local junior high school and baseball tryouts were the same week. I knew I had talent and enough talent to make the small town junior high baseball team. I went to tryouts wearing sweat pants and an appetite to make the team. The coach asked what elementary school I went to and I told him Leesburg elementary and asked where that was, and I wasn't certain, but at least I knew it was in Indiana. He scratched his head and asked where I was really from; I said Indiana and I currently lived in Old State Village Trailer park. I didn't get a single response, until I went to check the team roster on his classroom door and I did not see my name on the roster. I immediately jumped to a conclusion and was completely upset. The conclusion I jumped to was that I didn't make the team because no one knew who I was, I didn't have a name and I thought the coach was discriminating against me. I was the only person trying out that I didn't appear to be white. I perceived myself to be less superior than anyone on that team.

Looking back now, I was wrong, I was dead wrong. I don't know how I came to that conclusion. It never appeared to me that I might not have been as good as some of the other kids that made that team. I mean, that summer in Leesburg I made the all-star team and thought I was the most incredible player on earth. I perceived to be the best and I was wrong. I missed an open door of opportunity. Did I not give it my all? Did I blame all the other reasons for not making the team or the coach and other players? Did the coach ask me questions to see how I would interact with the team or to check my personality? These questions haunted me for most of childhood. I did not try out for that team again, nor did I consider that team to be that good. At the time I was cut, I had really negative feelings towards some of the kids on the team. Some of which I didn't even know. Look, this is the reality: I thought the kids that made the team were superior, rich, white, jocks, cools, and any other derogatory adjective I could conjure. I never once thought the kids just simply had better skill than I did. The irony is when I played summer ball a year later in Mattoon, I made the City all start team, and it was the same team as the junior high team, with one exception, me. Making the all-star team sent me down a path of feelings that I cannot deny. Now, I was in the same boat. Even though, it was derogatory before, now I was cool, a jock and maybe considered rich. Like the kids I loathed before, now I was in my own perception hell and I could be classified as the same as them. What a vicious circle. I thought nothing but bad things about these guys and now I was glad to be one of them. Poor perception causes terrible thoughts. If I was more concerned about what I could do to excel or to get better rather than to be concerned about another child's status amongst the schools elite I could have been on the junior high team. Yes, the same junior high team that has haunted me for all of these years. Even as I was moving around in high school and made various high school teams I would always look back at being cut on the junior high team as a moment of: drive. I told myself I would never get cut again. And, so I didn't. Yes being cut gave me drive, but it also provided clarity several years after that fateful day at the coach's classroom door. Those kids on the team, cut or not, still put their pants on the same way I do; one leg at time. Just because they live in nice houses and tried out in baseball pants, and I didn't, doesn't make them worse or better, in my perception it was always better. It is not their fault for living in a nice house or having baseball pants. My poor perception caused all of this turmoil. Without having to dive too much into self-esteem and the science behind it, can you imagine what being cut from a team sport would do to a young boy's self-esteem? At the time, it was the world, and that was my perception. Looking back, I played the victim really well. Never blaming myself for poor performance, but blaming everyone else for things I was jealous of. It was easier to blame and blame is a nasty roadblock.

I have worked over the years to remove any presupposed perceptions until I know completely, all of the circumstances behind any situation. I have always experienced that there is an answer behind any situation, you just have to remove any and all negative value perceptions. Approaching anything with negativity will almost certainly set you up for failure even before you try. One final note, when I joined the Marine Corps, I was under the perception that running 5 miles with full gear that weighed about 65 pounds was something that I could not do. That was my perception going in and I was already going to fail the test. The true test was not whether I could physically accomplish the run, but if I could perceive that I could do the run. I completed the run, passed the test and I opened the door of opportunity without any preconceived notion that I would fail.

CHAPTER 7

The Evolution of a Turn Around

"Live your beliefs and you can turn the world around."

–Henry David Thoreau

The sling shot effect, as I commonly refer to it, is the moment you realize you have to make a change. I tell students in my classes if you want to see change in the people around you, you must be first. Not to be confused with first in line, or first in competition, but first in change. You have to make a change in yourself if you expect it from others. The best approach is ask people around you, "if I can change one thing about myself, what would it be?" You shouldn't be surprised by their answers, but if you are, your perceptions of self and what others perceive aren't completely aligned.

In 2009 I had to make many changes. I slipped into a person that I never want to visit again. I was the egomaniacal-everyone-owes-me-something-guy. I had entitlementitus. A condition that at the time I was oblivious to. I had no idea that I was in a position of senior authority. Actually, the story is flipped, I pretended that I had senior authority, but it was never given. I expected it and didn't earn it. I believed that I was senior in my position with my company and that I was untouchable. Was I ever wrong. I had so much to learn. As I mentioned in the chapter for Ego I was closing many doors of opportunities simply because I thought I ruled the world.

Well, the next step was to figure it out. I learned the hard way, a slap in the face. I mean, I didn't get physically slapped in the face, but I darn near deserved it. I was awaken by a series of mistakes that crashed in on me and my family. It was a massive humbling event that made me realize that I was in a business to help people out, save lives and make a difference in the world. The only world I cared to make a difference in was my own.

To give you some examples of entitlementitus should be daunting, but the examples poured right onto the page and easily, I might add. So here you go!

I deserve to take some time off.
I deserve to be lazy.
Someone should make me breakfast.
I want to purchase whatever I want, whenever I want.
I deserve a fancy car for working so hard.

Are you starting to get the picture? No one will ever argue with you if you feel tired and want to rest, but the minute you say I deserve to sleep in, is entitlementitus. You should sleep in because you are tired, not because you told yourself you deserve it. Understanding if you have entitlementitus is the first step. You cannot have a turn around until you are willing to admit you have a problem. So, I told myself, after being told by Sheila that I had some things I need to work on. Who was I to argue? She was right and it was bad. So what I did was not rocket science. Actually, the concept is fairly simple.

Instead of saying "I" what I did was replace "I" with Sheila. Sheila deserves to sleep in, Sheila deserves a fancy car, Sheila deserves to take some time off. I immediately saw a transformation in everything I did and the people around me. It was absolutely humbling to know that I had so much work to do and a lot of making up. I cannot imagine what kind of person I was, to be around and to have her be put through the wringer was very disappointing to me. I don't hate much, but I hate it when she is upset, mad or disappointed. Sooner or later, I was so humbled that I blurted out the words, "I don't deserve you." Sheila was upset that I said it, but she was quick to say, that she loved me and I was being ridiculous. I meant what I said, and I evolved, actually, it was an evolution of a turn around. When will you have yours? The Core of Four can help you achieve an evolution. Before we get to The Core of Four, I have to say that if you are not willing to change, the rest of this book is not for you. You should put it down and not continue.

The rest of this book is about what you can do to perform change within yourself and to help yourself around other people. If you are willing or ready to help yourself and people around you, then I would encourage you to continue. You won't be disappointed.

CHAPTER 8

The Introduction to
The Core of Four

"Starting over isn't all that bad, because when you restart you get a chance to make things right."

—William "Jack" Jackson

I was golfing in Tucson with a good friend David Silva. I was hitting and the ball went to a location where there was a potential that I wouldn't find my ball. I hit a provisional ball just in case I couldn't find the first one. The second shot went right down the middle and even further than the original. Dave posed a question, which was more like a statement, "isn't the second shot always better?" It wasn't the first time I heard that because I hit quite a few bad "first" shots, but to do it all over again means you probably know what you needed to correct, which also means that you knew what you did to hit such a bad shot. I concluded, that we all don't usually get that second shot in life, but to do it all again you could correct what you did wrong. It is really easy for me to tell you that you should step up to the tee box and just hit without making any mistakes. Can you imagine if life was like that? This book is not about hitting a perfect shot each time, but how you recover to make par. In other words, if you hit an errant tee shot, can you still make it in the cup at par or better? It is **EXTREMELY** possible to make par even with a mistake or two. Professional golfers are good not because they are perfect, but they always seem to scramble and make par. They know they will hit a bad shot now and again and if you ever watch them play, they are good for a few bad shots each round. The end goal is putting together more good shots than bad.

Developing The Core of Four was a moment for me when I finally realized that I am not going to perfect the game of life (or golf for that matter), but to get good or better, I still needed to practice so the culmination and putting together The Core of Four took me a very long time. I knew practice was a big part of the whole plan, but how do I put it into motion?

It started in 2002 when I met Larry Wilson. He was present- ing at a conference in Mesa, Arizona and his presentation title was "Making Common Sense Common Practice." I thought it was a brilliant title and what he had to present wasn't new information but it was put together in such a fashion that people that were listening to him had their own "self" op- portunities to practice and get better for themselves. As the years progressed, I started to practice to curve my appetite to move fast, and drive aggressively. Although I can get better at both, at least I started working on it. Now, practice is great if you know what you need to practice on. Let's move forward to 2009. My wife was invited with a group of performers to sing at Carnegie Hall in New York City and earlier in late 2004 I heard a cliché in class when I was talking to someone about practice. Vern Vasquez a superintendent for the City of Phoenix Water Services asked me a question, "do you know how to get to Carnegie Hall?" I was dumbfounded and said, "I dunno." He replied, "practice." A huge light bulb clicked for me and I was certain that this was going to be used when I start to write my book. Let's get back to future in 2009. I was thinking of the "Vern Cliché" when I was walking with my wife and girls at ground zero near the World Trade Center construction. It finally all came to me. My wife was invited to sing at Carnegie Hall and she practiced hard to get there. I took a random photograph of the girls and they were perfectly framed in the photo with the construction activities in the background. See Photo Number 1.

I did not ask them to move perfectly into the photo but it made sense to me that people are the strong foundation of any building, foundation, or company. And if you want them to get good at what they do, you really have to frame them. Frame them? Yeah frame them. Not the whole, "I was framed" mentality because someone was blamed for someone else's behavior. No, frame them. Put them in the frame so the picture becomes clear. How do we frame someone?

Photo Number 1

Perfect Practice. Now, I had one of the elements of the Core of Four. You might be asking why perfect practice? You won't get any better if you are practicing poorly. When I was younger, I was in the batting cages and my dad saw that I was half swinging to make contact without taking a full swing. He pulled me out of the cages and said to me, "did your coach tell you that practice makes perfect?" I replied quizzically, "yes." He sharply returned, "He is lying." Again, I was confused, but he completed his point by saying, "practice does not perfect if you are going to half swing." "You need perfect practice to make perfect and if you continue to practice with a half swing you will play with a half swing." Those comments er, more like coaching statements, were so profound they stuck with me forever. He was right! If you practice poorly, you will perform poorly. Conversely, if you practice perfectly you will perform as perfect as you practice. It is very difficult for me to say that you can perform perfectly because if performance was perfect, then everything would be perfect. The problem is simple and that is where Motivation, Accountability and Exercising Discipline come in. Athletes that get paid millions of dollars are being paid to execute in their respective performance arena. Whether it is a football field, a soccer pitch, a hockey rink, or a racket ball court, athletes have to perform to win and competition drives performance. Competition equals **motivation**. If you play for a team you are **accountable** to your team and coaches. Finally, if you want to excel or improve you need to **exercise discipline**. To put them into a different order, Motivation, Accountability, Practice Perfectly, Exercise Discipline spells out the acronym MAPPED. It is the main reason this book is put together and it boils down to asking yourself one question. Have you M.A.P.P.E.D. out your day?

CHAPTER 9

Motivation

"Around here however, we don't look backwards very long. We keep moving forward opening new doors and doing new things because we're curious and curiosity keeps leading us down new paths."

— Walt Disney

I was watching a Disney movie with my girls called "Meet the Robinson's" and at the end of the movie this Walt Disney quote came on and both me and the girls started tearing up. This man who had great triumphs, yet, had even greater setbacks, but he just kept moving forward. He was motivated by something until eventually he became successful. He has endured so much pain but he kept moving forward. He was motivated far greater than the pain he experienced in his past. I always worried about showing my daughters too much television as they grew up and along with that, maybe showing them too many movies. I am glad we watched the Disney movies together. They all (every single one of them) have special meaning to our family. We have a huge collection of Walt Disney movies, which for some reason, Courtney has claimed as her own. These movies were a part of Courtney and to some extent Camryn's up-bringing. As Camryn got older she started gaining more of an interest in Japanese Animation commonly referred to Anime and less of a Disney affinity. The example of the two girls liking different animation is a great example of uniqueness and shows that different things can motivate people. I never knew how much of an impact the Disney organization would have on my girls but they were huge. Walt Disney wanted to make a place for his children to enjoy and in his vision he created Disneyland but his prime motivator was his children. His legacy has really made Disney, the company, become successful themselves and it really boils down to motivation. What motivated Walt Disney to succeed? Was it his family? Was it his desire for animation to become main-stream? Was it money? If you read all the biographies written about Walt you get a strong sense that Walt wanted to make a difference in all of our lives and I truly believe he has accomplished that. I wouldn't expect that you would want to achieve epic Disney success, but success nonetheless. The first letter of the Core of Four is the letter M. You need to stop what you are doing and just ask yourself, "What motivates YOU?" If you are wondering what others are saying what motivates them, then I have collected a list from polling audiences at conferences I have spoken at in the last 15 years. Here are what my attendees are saying motivates them:

1. Money;
2. Keeping their word for commitment;
3. Supporting non-work related hobbies like softball, golf, hunting, etc.;
4. They love their job;
5. They love the people they work with;
6. Supporting a bad habit;
7. Community activities like volunteering on housing associations, children's groups, etc.;
8. Gaining prestige from their performance;
9. Being recognized
10. The greater good;
11. Religious faith;
12. To win a game;
13. Watching TV;
14. Music;
15. Friends;
16. Neighbors;
17. Party's
18. Curiosity;
19. Alcohol, yes someone said that;
20. The alarm clock said it was time to get up, therefore the alarm clock was motivating;
21. And finally, the most popular answer to the question is Family.

I have gathered data on what would be the most popular, by gauging my audience responses at conferences. Family has always been a huge motivator for people when it comes to decision-making. Part of the decisions we make solely circle around motivation only. We sometimes skip other factors like The Doors of Opportunity and the rest of the Core of Four. If family is the sole motivator, your intent will be golden, however mistakes play a big part if you don't finish making the complete decision. For example, for a family that is living paycheck to paycheck and the bread-winner of the family gets laid off from their job there might be an increased opportunity to skip accountability steps to continue providing for the family. The bread-winner of the family might be motivated to feed the family, so motivated that they take steps to steal or shortcut the system to get food for the family. Survival instincts will certainly kick in, but there are better ways than to steal or shortcut the system.

I was in Myrtle Beach, South Carolina for a conference and created a poll for some of the answers you might see in this book. One of the questions was personal, but I asked and the answers might surprise you. I won't bore you with the details but I want to give you one final word of wisdom. An idea that was given to me by a student that completely rings true for me is to keep my word. Have you ever promised to do something and forgot to do it? If you forgot to do something as easy as picking up milk on your way home, you feel horrible when you are given the reminder. I found that what happens next usually defines what motivates you. Instantly, if you feel horrible, you wanted to keep your word and you were equally motivated to get the milk, but now want to do it even more. If you are one of the folks that say, ehh whatever, you may not be motivated to go and get the milk you forgot to pick up in the first place. This same mentality can be carried over into all aspects of your life. Consider all the things you have forgotten to do. How many are there? The best anecdote for this unfortunate series of events is that you can use your forgetfulness as a source of pure self-motivation. In other words, if you know you are forgetful the best thing for you or me to do, is to just get it done right away or to do something that will aide your memory. Larry has always told me it is better to do something to aide in your memory to help fight complacency. The same goes with forgetting to do something. I forget things all the time and I just convert forgetfulness into immediate action and take care of business right away! What a great motivator. You know come to think of it, if you get things done right away you might be able to keep your word. Remember the student in Myrtle Beach? Keeping their word was the one thing that motivated them. Do you know what motivates you? Even if you know some personal motivators, it wouldn't hurt to take a new inventory. Ask yourself this question at least daily. Write them down and remind yourself what they are. After you determine what motivates you, accountability is the next step. Who are you accountable to? If you are not accountable to someone or a team, then be accountable to yourself.

Take a moment to provide a personal inventory of what motivates you and list them below.

1)_____

2)_____

3)_____

4)_____

5)_____

6)_____

CHAPTER 10

Accountability

"If you could kick the person in the pants responsible for most of your trouble, you wouldn't sit for a month."

Theodore Roosevelt

In early 2002 the City of San Diego had a struggle with their municipal employees performing minimal amounts of work. The employees would work on two or three work orders after being issued several. Once they finished with just the two, the entitled employees would congregate at the local park and rest (not work) in their city issued vehicles. A local news channel captured the events for several months and documented each time the employees would gather. After five months into the investigation the news channel broadcasted the report. Throughout the investigative reporting, not once did the journalist mention the lack of accountability. The report only mentioned the amount of money San Diegans were spending on resting employees and not working employees. The best part of the newscast was you didn't need anyone telling you there was a severe lack of accountability. In this moment no one needed to say it because it was implied. These employees were accountable to the citizens of San Diego paying for City related services like trash, water and sewer fees. Since accountability did not motivate employees to perform their functions for what they were being paid for and handsomely, I must add; they felt compelled to take advantage of trust and it showed a complete disregard to the policies and procedures already in place.

Kevin Cobb mentioned to me some time ago in Las Vegas that most people under our current and last government administration will be playing the blame game for a very long time. Blame is such a big game right now. There is no personal accountability for anyone's actions in the United States government. I am not going to dive into political affiliations right now, but I do want to bring something up that has been plaguing me since after the elections in 2000. Our society is so litigious that we have to find the blame in almost everything. I am a safety professional and even when there is an injury or mishap that causes property damage, there is a root cause or fault tree analysis performed. The root cause analysis is performed to find the end causes, or basically, find blame. The analysis is used to prevent the reoccurrence in the future, but it has been used in a court of law for liability, civilly and criminally. I know it sounds so easy for me to sit here and tell you to take accountability for your actions whether you were prepared for the outcome of your actions or not. Even in marriage, I have learned that I am the one that usually screws up so I have already decided for arguments sake that I am pre-screwed up. You would not even know how much time this saves. I have shifted my thought process with the What Would Sheila Do question before any decision I make. I mean I would usually call and ask Sheila her opinion on something and I would already know what her answer would be. She would become my moral compass on most decisions I would make, but all this means is I have great respect and admiration for her and I am accountable to my family and moreover, her, Sheila. I remember being in the military and some of the other married guys would always call me whipped or a wimp, or they would want to go do guy things and jokingly ask me if I could get a "kitchen pass." I mean I used to ask Sheila about almost everything. Mostly, I would ask because at the time I was young and I didn't have much confidence in my decision-making skills.

The Military has taught me so much that I am grateful for the life lessons more so than the skill (job) lessons. I have learned to become accountable for my actions via the military. I got into so much trouble when I was on active duty. I thought it was normal to get into trouble as a Marine, but I was the only person that thought that. I had no idea how to handle my finances, my responsibilities or my behavior around women. But the Marine Corps made me realize, the really hard way, that I was accountable to God, Corps and Country and yes in that order. When I met Sheila it all changed personally because she was such a straight shooter and I learned to come around. To give you some history at some of the mistakes I made in the Marine Corps I will start off with writing bad checks. When I returned from Operation Desert Storm/Shield I thought I had a ton of money in the bank and I could just write checks without balancing a check book. Man, was I ever wrong. I know I learned how to balance a check book in 6th grade, but I never put its practical use in practice for myself. 14 days restricted duty and barracks duty was a result of writing a couple of bad checks. Wow! I received what the military calls office hours and reported to my company commander. When I stepped into his office, I finally realized what I did and the magnitude of my actions. My company commander held me responsible for those checks and ordered me to pay the money, and handed out my "sentence." Of course, my sentence included the restrictions but also forced me to take a class on personal finance through the Marine Corps Institute. During the restriction I was caught with a young lady in my room at the barrakcs I was restricted to. She was found during a routine Wednesday morning fire alarm in the barracks. 14 more days restricted duty and complete barracks lockdown was the result of this this punishment. In between restriction assignments was when I met Sheila. I was so head over heals that I didn't have time to make any more mistakes. Our chance meeting was a story for a Nicolas Sparks novel. I was in a car with three other friends and she was driving her car with her sister and cousin. Sheila followed us into the parking lot of the Del Mar Enlisted men's club. We did not know that they were following us, but we went ahead and got into line for the military only. There was another line for military sponsors of civilians. That is when Sheila, her sister and cousin asked us to sign them in. I was delighted they asked and had my eyes fixated on Sheila. I suggested that my three friends sign them in and I would go into the club and scope it out first. I didn't realize that I was being mean and self-centered when I met her, but I can see her point now. After cruising the inside first, I came back out to the sponsor line and hung out with them. The rest is history and we hit off. I did have to serve my restriction after we met. I even snuck out of barracks restriction to have dinner and play tennis with Sheila. I would have done anything for the chance to see her again. I love her so much, that I am accountable to her for everything I do.

Now that we have been together for over 27 years, I have learned that if Sheila would say yes or no to a question, that's it. Just let it be. Interestingly enough, there have been times that I have wanted something so badly that according to Sheila, I would "wear" her down until I got my way. I suppose an example would be warranted here. In 2005 I wanted the new Xbox 360 video game console so badly. Sheila insisted that it wasn't a good idea, but I insisted and continued to she finally said, "fine just leave me alone." Was I that much of a child to wear her down like that? Yes, is the answer. I have got to fight that urge or the road block of temptation especially when I am accountable to someone else other than myself. In this case, I have learned if I am accountable to Sheila and the family, I should be accountable to myself and in turn accountable for all of my actions. Whether my actions are good or bad in terms of outcomes, I should be accountable for them all.

In the past I have had difficulty being accountable for my actions and in some cases would place blame on others or even on the situation. It is far more convenient to place blame to reflect internally. If I made a great decision, I wanted all the accolades but when it came to making a mistake I wanted to be very far away from that accountability. I just don't like being the bad person. But sometimes in life you have to be the bad person even in poor judgment. I have gained a different perspective in life even with all the disastrous mistakes I have made. Someone has to answer for them, and I have learned to take that responsibility especially if it's mine to take. One final note about accountability, one of the huge turning points for me was when I started to place blame towards me for anything that goes wrong or right. What it does for me, blame or not, is figure out if there is something else I could have done better. I figured out that I could always do better and if everyone worked at getting better all the time then you wouldn't have to be accountable to anyone but yourself.

After you determine what motivates you, you now have to ask yourself, "Who are you accountable to?" Even if you have no one you are accountable you will still need to be accountable to yourself. Make decisions as if you have other people you will impact after your decision is made. What will the impact be and how would affect others? If you ask this question, you will find out to whom you are accountable to. I always ask what would Sheila do? I usually find my answer instantly.

You can ask who you should be accountable to, but you really don't need to. Be accountable to you.

CHAPTER 11

Practice Perfectly

"Practice does not make perfect, perfect
practice makes perfect."

–Curt Bottorff

I was in a batting cage and my dad pulled me out of the cage and asked if I would bat left handed. I was so scared that I would look silly so when I turned around and batted left handed I would half swing just to make contact with the ball. He was immediately disappointed and pulled me back out of the cages. He asked me if my coach ever told me that practice makes perfect and I was absolutely confused. I replied, "yes sir." He displayed a bit of amusement and said, "he was lying." I was even more confused. He went on to further coach and said, "practice does not make perfect, perfect practice makes perfect." He continued, "if you practice making half swings in the cage, you will make half swings when it comes to playing a game." So, it was when I was 8 years old, that I learned to practice perfectly. You could consider being in the batting cage as part of preparing for life and life is the game.

I make a profound statement at all of my speaking engagements, "your personal safety behavior is a direct reflection of your driving behavior when you are alone." How do you drive? Do you ever say, I need to get better at this or that? I make this statement all the time but I find myself making most of my mistakes when I drive the car. I really need to practice better, or in this case practice something perfectly. Poor practice could contribute to poor performance and this concept is not new. The most difficult part about practicing perfectly is the roadblocks that we face each and every day. It is within this chapter that I have found most of my solace in regards to transferring roadblocks into doors of opportunity. The major roadblocks that have caused me to practice the most with are my temptations and ego. Some of the challenges in our society include the need to exercise. We spend more time with excuses to not exercise that we already justify why we won't practice getting healthier. This common roadblock is laziness or convenience.

I face the same roadblock but it is not my worst. I commonly tell myself that I have no time, I'm too tired, I travel too much to carry equipment to work out, the hotel does not have an exercise facility, etc. etc. etc. Does any of this sound familiar? Part of the reason that the fit people in society are so fit is because they practice perfectly, and more importantly, we all want to be fit but what are we doing about it? One more

PRACTICE PERFECTLY

example I can give you is what I learned in the SafeStart process. When attending a SafeStart session one of the key components is to work on your safety related habits. If you truly work on them (practice perfectly) you will get better at minimizing critical errors, which could get you hurt. When I was exposed to SafeStart in 2002 Larry told me that I could do a better job for myself if I were to immediately work on my safety related habits. One of the habits listed in the course was to turn and look before moving your body, eyes or car. When I saw this, I immediately tried to work on it (practice perfectly). It is still a work in progress but when I realized that I was not turning and looking and how many times a day I was doing this it made me want to get better.

The first step in the mode of perfect practice is to ask yourself what do you need the most practice with. I made a list of things that I need to practice with and they weren't in any particular order. Once I had them written down, I started to systematically prioritize the list. With your list, it can be a bad habit you need to work on or working closer with your children or getting out there and help your community by volunteering in a local organization. Whatever your list is populated with, prioritizing the list will help identify what is really important to you. Work on the first two or three items on the list and eventually work your way down the list with the others. Please remember this chapter is not about just practicing, but to practice perfectly. If you practice perfectly you can achieve success specifically with the items you are motivated by and ultimately you will meet requirements for those you have to be accountable to. Below is my

... 63 ...

list I created for things I wanted to get better at. The list is a current work in progress and it changes from time to time and it depends on what I am motivated by at any particular point in time. Your list may be different and we may match, but it is ok to have your list change when your motivation changes over time.

Tim's Personal Practice List

1. Better communication with Sheila.
2. Better communication with my children.
3. Get better with my aggressive driving.
4. Get more organized with my travel arrangements.
5. Work on turning and looking before I move my body and car.
6. Be the best safety professional I can be.
7. Finish writing the Core of Four.
8. Help mentor our consultants.
9. Spend more time at home.
10. Get better sleep
11. Volunteer more with my local and regional areas of the American Society of Safety Professionals (ASSP).
12. Work on becoming a good leader within the ASSP to help shape the safety profession.
13. Work with Larry on the new exciting things coming out for SafeStart.
14. Show unconditional love for my family.

This list is not all inclusive and continues to change from time to time based on my individual needs. Your needs will change from time to time, but whatever is on your list don't just practice them, practice them perfectly.

The Magnificent Case of Captain LaSalle

Captain Chris LaSalle was getting ready to go to Pam's 20-year high school class reunion. Little did Chris know this 20-year reunion would shape his post Marine Corps life. Chris and Pam travelled from New Bern, North Carolina to San Diego to attend this reunion. They both met and were married in San Diego just after Chris graduated Marine Corps Boot Camp. Chris was uncertain about what he was going to do after he retired from the Marine Corps. He was quite open for anything that would provide for his family over what he earned from the Marine Corps retirement. For quite some time Pam, his wife, was in contact with a friend who was also in the same graduating class as Pam. Sheila, Pam's friend, had planned on meeting Chris and Pam during the reunion, as they have not seen each other for several years. The three of them emerged from the crowd with Sheila's husband in tow. Sheila's husband happened to be a Marine Veteran too. Although, Chris was not quite separated from the Marine Corps yet, he was already actively looking for opportunities and when he met Sheila's husband, they hit it off immediately. I was Sheila's husband. Chris and I got to talking about what his aspirations were and he mentioned to me that public speaking was not one of them. I just recently learned that aspirations were the highest level we are all willing to go given failure. Public speaking was not an option, or so he thought. We laughed and joked for quite a while and eventually his personality was a great asset. I mentioned to Chris that he has what it takes to be a SafeStart consultant with overflowing integrity and incredible desire to succeed. I recommended to Chris that he take the next steps and get ready to become a consultant. Well, Chris took the necessary steps to start down the path of retirement from the Marine Corps. Prior to his retirement he also started the process of becoming a consultant. As this story ends, my point begins. Chris was NOT a public speaker and was rough around the edges. I took him to Los Angeles to train him and to also give him a shot at "live rounds" in front of a very important customer. What I wasn't sure of is how much practice Chris was able to get under his belt before I threw him under the fire in L.A. Well, Chris wasn't perfect, but he knew the material and must have spent countless hours preparing and practicing perfectly. I have to give him credit because I was unclear if personality would win over lack of skill. Chris had both. Jack Jackson spent the majority and remainder of time training and coaching Chris after we all left L.A. After talking to Jack, he mentions the amount of work Chris has done to get to where he is now. The magnificent case of Captain LaSalle is a story that needs to be shared. In my many years working in the safety business, I have found that more than 95% of the people practicing safety or health can learn the business through training and experience. Standing in front of a group of people takes a talent that most cannot succeed in without training and experience or perfect practice. You can practice all you want, but drive and interest need to be at the front of the car because your skill will take a back seat especially after you beat yourself up. Captain LaSalle had drive and interest but what helped him move that to the front of the car was his ability to practice perfectly.

CHAPTER 12

Exercise Discipline

"If you don't discipline yourself someone else will."

– Samuel L. Jackson

Why would my berm mate and I build a fox hole to help us stay awake? It was a decision to maintain discipline. Nothing happened that night and of course the perfect recipe was in the mix for a Marine to fall asleep at his post, but there was no excuse. I have beat myself up over this incident for years. No one even knows this story, not even Sheila. I am so embarrassed about it and it is something that I am not proud about. So, I work extremely hard to avoid situations when I know I am overly tired, like avoiding driving or something with that much hazardous energy. I will tell you this, there have been many occasions in my travels where I have arrived on a really late flight and had to drive 2 or 3 hours to arrive at a hotel, only having to teach an 8 hour class the next day. The discipline part is what you do before you make any type of mistake. In other words, avoid the mistake or performance error by maintaining or exercising discipline.

One of the greatest things that has happened to me is Sheila. Recently Sheila has started a fitness company and she isn't a personal trainer per se, but she is coaching other people to help make better fitness and nutrition decisions. She is 100% absolutely committed to see her students/clients/friends achieve success, but the best part about it is she is doing it for herself too. She has really just made me super proud with her personal discipline to get her fitness in check and she religiously works out and if she misses a workout because she is ill or something comes up, she makes it up by doubling her next day work out. I found it really cool that she gets angry if she misses a workout. I actually rejoice when I miss a workout (lack of exercising discipline). I know I need to get into shape and I have been working hard to get there, but the difference between me and her is I attach myself to an excuse quickly to avoid having to do something that is hard like exercising. Here is a perfect example, I travel for work and I arrive at my destinations late and sometimes at the funkiest hours. Since I was traveling, there is no way that I could work out. That couldn't be further from the truth. The fact of the matter is, I could have worked out when I woke up, or when I land regardless of the time. I could do something. I could exercise discipline and just get it done. It is so much easier to find the excuse (convenience) than it is to complete the task.

One of the best things that have worked out for me is if I know something needs to be done, I do it as soon as it is brought to my attention. Throughout the years, I do not like to forget important things and as I mentioned, your brain is not a fail safe device for remembering every important thing. So the discipline to do it right away or doing something to aide your memory assists you in decision making. You have a door of opportunity and if you pass it up, you are not exercising discipline. Also, if you absolutely cannot get something done that needs to be done, make yourself accountable to get it done. I am certain if it crossed your mind, you probably don't need the motivation answer questioned. If you get that call to get milk on your way home from work, just do it right away. I mean do it at the first store you see. If you wait for the grocery store that is closest to your house you may forget. Doing it right away is a great way to condition yourself to better exercise discipline. Procrastination is the king of injecting poor discipline. The less you put things off, the more disciplined you will remain. I want to finish this chapter with a more recent event that has happened at our house. At the time of writing this chapter, my niece Ashlee and youngest daughter Camryn are still at the house and have common chores. One of the chores is to put the dishes away when they are done being cleaned in the dishwasher. After several requests from me or Sheila telling the kids to come and do their dishes it turns into a shouting match. One of the things that Sheila or I can't do is put the dirty dishes into the dishwasher until it has been emptied. Eventually, I get tired of waiting so I end up putting the dishes away. The decision to put them away is mostly impatience and my distaste for clutter. I am of the school if it needs to be done then someone needs to do it as opposed to waiting for someone to do it. What the girls need to realize is that there is a fair bit of team work and we are further enabling their ability to procrastinate. We aren't teaching them anything about discipline, but yelling at them for our impatience. I have to be more skilled in the patience arena and understand that I am not helping them build better discipline; I am actually helping them develop poor discipline. One of the things we do as society is when we speak of discipline we speak of it with a ton of negative connotation. For example, "if you don't put your dishes away you will be grounded for life!" If we start speaking of discipline in positive terms, we just may be able to get folks to better exercise discipline for themselves. Exercising discipline is a good thing, not a bad thing.

The only true way to explain the difficulties of exercising discipline is to examine your driving behavior. As I said earlier it is so much easier to blame the other person than to introspectively assume the blame. The next time you get angry or disappointed in another driver you have to stop yourself internally and reverse the roles. Put yourself in the blame category and say, "what can I do better myself." I have this internal fight every time I get into the car and it never seems to resolve itself until I place blame on myself regardless if I am to blame or not. It automatically forces me back into the moment. Sheila would tell you that I still have a lot of work to do in this category but for me exercising discipline is just the beginning. Don't forget that the shortest distance between beginning and success is discipline.

CHAPTER 13

Have you M.A.P.P.E.D. Out Your Day?

> *"Life is one amazing, sweet song, so let's get the music started."*
>
> – Ronald Reagan

Up until this point you have heard many stories and anecdotes from my past that has helped shaped my foundation to success with success (overcoming roadblocks.) Please make a note that I stated success and not perfection. I already know that if I was able to perfect anything, I would not be able to keep up with demands for this book, that goes for any one else too. What I do know, is if you keep working at The Core of Four you can only get better with a great number of things. Originally I intended this book to be for safety professionals and how they can approach their business or customers. But the book has become much more than a safety professional self help book. I need to go back to my roots, to introduce the final chapter of this book.

Imagine you are a safety professional and your sole responsibility is to prevent injuries and accidents to employees at your workplace. Imagine, also, that you have employees who have a blatant disregard for the procedures and policies that were set forth to also help prevent injuries. As a safety professional you have to communicate with them and tell them to follow the requirements, put on their safety glasses, teach them things to remind them to follow procedures, perform hands on demonstrations, do onsite inspections, audits and all the enforcement that goes with being the best safety professional you can be. It is perception that kills the best of intentions. If you ask anyone what they perceive safety as, most respond with, "waste of time," "not fun at all," "hardly any benefit," "man, they are all Nazis," "yeah, I have to go to another safety class," "this pretty much sucks." Now don't get me wrong you will find the occasional person that will give you the positive aspects of a safety professional but that is rare. Why do you suppose people (most people) have a hard time with proactive safety? I have a hunch, but let me set the mood. You are driving down your favorite stretch of highway and you notice a cop gauging your speed on a speed gun and you immediately check your speed and you see that you are actually going the speed limit but the cop puts the gun down and immediately turns on the lights, speeds up and tries to catch up with you. You are now bewildered and unsure if you did anything. You tell yourself, that you were comfortably going the speed limit and that you certainly didn't do anything wrong. But, there it is again, that super un-casual uncertainty if you did anything wrong. You pull over and the cop is behind you lights flashing and the super long pause before the driver side door opens with your impending doom. The police officer steps his first step out of the car door and you get anxiety like you just committed the biggest crime of the century. You are now flip flopping back and forth with your own insecurities and you question your lane changes, your turning signal use, the speed through a school zone, the seat belt, cell phone was down, there was no one in the car who didn't have their seat belt on, you check and double check. Your procedure inventory is complete and you are now certain you were following all standards, policies and procedures. Your window is still up and the officer approaches your car, he taps on your window with his extremely large flashlight and you hesitantly roll the wind down. You are not sure if you are to engage the conversation or wait to let the officer chime in, so you wait and it is an uncomfortable pause. The officer places his hands on his belt as if he was from the 1950's filming a western and you anticipate he will start every sentence with the word "howdy pard-ner." After he places his hands on his belt he stares off in the distance and speaks the words, "do you know why I pulled you over?" He never makes any eye contact with you and you stumble for words. Is the image set in your mind? Before I continue, I want you to really think of this place. Think of it in terms if you have ever been in this position. If you have never been in this position, you have been very fortunate, lucky or you have really good driving skills. Now that the stage is set, how do you feel? Or you put off by the officer? Or you upset that your day has been delayed? Are you still in quiz land? Are you wondering what you did wrong? Are you perplexed by his question of why he pulled you over? Do you just simply hate cops? Do you have an experience that you are pulling into your immediate present that has tainted your view of being pulled over? There could be a million questions. But immediately we forget what police officers are for and we just want to think of all the negatives. This is immediately what happens with safety professionals in the workplace. When employees are in front of (notice my exclusion of the word confronted) a safety professional the conversation is usually about safety behavior which quickly turns into, you didn't do this, or you didn't do that, or you need to get better at this. My friend and colleague Kevin Cobb always asks a question at our public workshops. His question, "When was the last time you gave your spouse any feedback on their behavior?" He quickly adds, "was that the last bit of feedback you will ever give?" It's funny to think about but it is true! So let's go back to the police officer standing at your window. You reply back to the officer, "no, but I am sure you are going to tell me why you pulled me over." Probably not the best set of words and most certainly not the sweetest of tones, but you continue and say, "what did I do now?" You are automatically guilty for something you didn't even do! The officer replies, "well I was clocking you back there on radar and it said you were actually going the speed limit and I wanted to thank you for your efforts and going the speed limit." Your jaw drops and you are instantly thinking how you messed that up slipping into sarcasm and negativity. Yeah, that's right negativity. Has there ever been a documented time where a police officer pulls anyone over for actually doing the right thing? No and back to the problem at hand. It is perceived that safety professionals/police officers are enforcement agents and spend their time "policing" things up. What if we were to create a paradigm that would shift the entire world. I mean, could you imagine saying, "oh cool the police are here, I must have done something right." It is a different way to think, but it is a start. So to get started, ask yourself each and every day, "Have I MAPPED out my day?" It is akin to skipping. I don't know what it is, but every time I skip, I smile. If you positively start your day out, you almost don't have any time to think negatively. Motivation can ultimately be the best way to get started with a positive launch to your day. You know what motivates you, why don't you cater to what you are motivated by? Are you motivated by negativity? I don't think so and if you are, there are so many things in life that you are missing and life will simply pass you by. If anything, try and keep your word, that will motivate you to get things done. Don't forget the roadblocks to success, or if you are looking at it with a positive spin, don't waste an open door of opportunity.

Accountability is the toughest of the Core of Four to figure out, but you won't have to spend too much time, because at the 10,000 foot level you should, at the very least, be accountable to yourself. Remember that pride and ego usually are the biggest roadblocks and can cause some serious damage to your self-esteem. Damage to the self-esteem can inflict much harm to accomplishing tasks that you are motivated to complete. Understanding the path to accountability is just the beginning but achieving it takes a bit of work. Be accountable to yourself first then you can be accountable to all others. Don't forget it is easier to place blame as opposed to absorbing blame. If you absorb blame you will always be looking at what you need to fix instead of telling others what they need to fix. Even when you know you haven't done anything, you can still always ask yourself, what do I need to do to be better? If you are ok with mediocrity and status quo, unfortunately then, status quo is all you will see around you. If you hold yourself accountable for you, it is highly likely you will get better, especially with perfect practice.

Perfect practice was not a term I understood at a younger age, but I did know that practice was important if you want to get good at whatever you are practicing. No, this is nothing new, however what was new to me was learning the skill to practice perfectly. With Sheila's invitation to Carnegie Hall the cliché became apparent. I finally understood what it meant to get to Carnegie Hall. Watching Sheila practice and practice hard and practice perfectly showed me something. I only recognized it a year or two later, but I recognized it and she worked really hard. It is counterproductive to go to practice and not work hard or practice perfectly. Give it a shot. What have you got to lose? Time? Money? Effort? Think about all you could lose if you were to practice poorly and your performance shows terrible results. What did you lose? That is a much different question so if you were prepared for what you could lose wouldn't you want to perform to the best of your ability to avoid any potential unwanted loss? Perfect practice makes perfect cents. That is not a typo.

As this chapter and book comes to a close it is fitting that we end with exercising discipline. There are so many ways to exercise discipline but the best way is to discipline yourself in your own way. In other words you have to create a path that you stick to whilst not being afraid of the journey. The best advise I ever received was from a Marine Corps drill instructor. Sergeant Jackson told me that if I ever wanted to finish a 5 mile run that I had to commit to it and never give up. The most important part of the conversation was commitment. He further went on to tell me that you will stumble but if you stay down you will never get up. So he completed the conversation with saying stay up and never get down. If you get knocked down get up no matter how much it hurts. The part of this conversation that directly relates to discipline is getting up. It is so much more convenient to stay down when you are hurt but the will and the energy you muster up must come from your heart and this is the point of discipline. Use your heart as a turning signal. It usually will guide you in the right direction.

Before you begin your day you have to ask, "Have I MAPPED out my day?

What are you **M**otivated by?

Who are you **A**ccountable to?

Will you **P**ractice **P**erfectly?

How will you **E**xercise **D**iscipline?

The Core of Four

CPSIA information can be obtained
at www.ICGtesting.com
Printed in the USA
FSHW020742091019

9 781977 210876